SPLISH! SPLASH!

ANIMAL BATHS

SPLISH!
SPLASH!

ANIMAL BATHS

by April Pulley Sayre

THE MILLBROOK PRESS
BROOKFIELD , CONNECTICUT

Splish, splash, take a bath. Brush your teeth clean.

And think of the animals.

They clean themselves, too.

Squirt! An elephant sprays water over its back. Squiiiiiirt! Baby will get a shower, too.

Pigs take their
baths in thick,
brown mud.
They soak, slog, snort
...and seem to smile.
Mud cools their skin.
And best of all, it gets
rid of itches, as well.

Birds take baths in puddles. Or shower under sprinklers or waterfalls. Once clean, they preen—smoothing, fluffing, and straightening their feathers. That's like hair brushing for you.

Ducks do extra work. They spread oil on their feathers. This special oil waterproofs them. Without it, ducks would get soggy and cold…which wouldn't be *ducky* at all!

Horses take baths—but not the bathtub
kind. They take baths in dust, instead. Roll,
roll…rolling in dirt scrubs off sweat and insects.
And then—shake! The dirt really flies.

(Speaking of flies,
a fly can clean itself,
too—with its handy,
spongelike tongue!)

Bears have long fur that gets itchy and full of insects.
To scratch itches, a bear rubs against a tree.
Bears also take dust baths. They roll in dirt.
Or they swim and splash in a wide, cool stream.

Even the king of beasts can get
beastly dirty. So lions do what house
cats do. They lick their long fur clean.
But even a lion's tongue can't reach the
back of its head...so it licks a paw and
rubs it over its head and ears.

A comb might come in handy for cleaning a chimpanzee's fur. But chimps don't have combs, so fingers work fine. Chimps bite and pull bugs and leaves from their family's and friends' fur. What are good buddies for?

Oxpeckers, a type of bird, spend their time hanging around. Where? On the bodies of giraffes. Giraffes don't seem to mind. Oxpeckers peck away ticks. They get a meal, and the giraffe gets clean.

Hippos have helpers, too. But these helpers are underwater, in the rivers and ponds where hippos wade. Fish nibble algae off a hippo's skin. Does it tickle the hippo? Only hippos know. And they won't say.

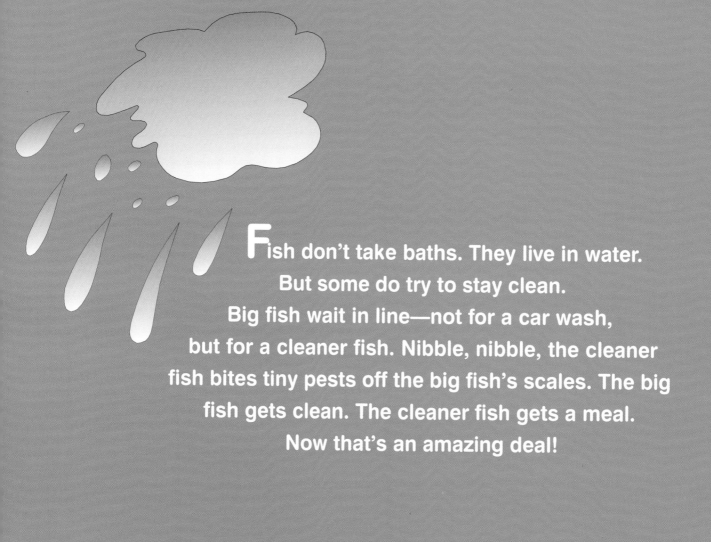

Fish don't take baths. They live in water.
But some do try to stay clean.
Big fish wait in line—not for a car wash,
but for a cleaner fish. Nibble, nibble, the cleaner
fish bites tiny pests off the big fish's scales. The big
fish gets clean. The cleaner fish gets a meal.
Now that's an amazing deal!

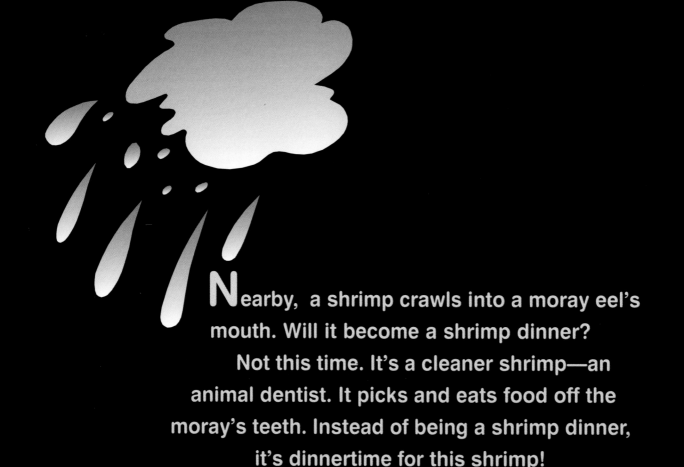

earby, a shrimp crawls into a moray eel's
mouth. Will it become a shrimp dinner?
Not this time. It's a cleaner shrimp—an
animal dentist. It picks and eats food off the
moray's teeth. Instead of being a shrimp dinner,
it's dinnertime for this shrimp!

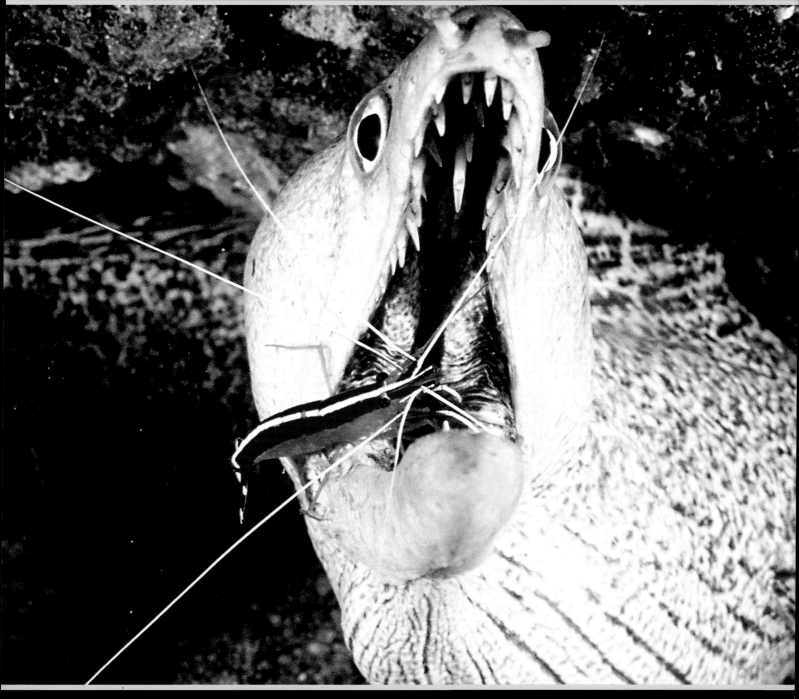

Now that you've heard about animal
baths and animal dentists, and how animals
splish, splash, peck, and preen...
it's time to take *your* bath. Splish and
splash. And think of the animals. They,
too, are getting clean.

PLACES FOR ANIMAL BATHS

You can observe animals taking water or dust baths. Look under sprinklers and in puddles after a rain. Late afternoon is an especially good time to see birds bathing. You may also see birds fluttering their wings among leaves wet with rain or dew. This is a kind of bathing, too.

Keep an eye out for dusty spots—empty lots, bare places in a lawn, or bare dirt under shrubs and trees. Birds often take dust baths in these places.

You can also make special places for animals to bathe. You need a front yard, backyard, schoolyard, or other place. First, ask the owner of the spot for permission to use it. Talk about your plans before you begin. You could try some of the following projects:

- In the late afternoon, set up a sprinkler. It's best if the sprinkler is watering a lawn, shrub, or tree. Light, misty sprinkles are best. Sometimes birds will come and shower in the sprinkler's spray.

- Make a small birdbath or wildlife pool. A birdbath needs to be only 2 feet (0.6 meter) or so in diameter, and 2 to 4 inches (5 to 10 centimeters) deep. A trash-can lid, turned upside down and filled with water, does the job just fine. A broad, shallow pan will work, too. You can also buy a birdbath at a gardening store. Although many birdbaths are set on pedestals, they can also be kept on the ground.

  You can make a wildlife pool by digging a shallow hole in the ground, lining it with plastic, then filling it with water. Remember: Deeper is not better. Small birds and other animals need shallow water for bathing.

- If you don't have an area where birds can take dust baths, you can create your own. It needs to be only about a foot in diameter. Look for a place that already has very few plants. Remove any that are left. Use a rake or other tool to scratch the dust into a fine powder. Then watch and see if birds use the spot.

For my nieces and nephews:

Turner & Winston & Elizabeth & Virginia

Cover photograph (brown bear) courtesy of Peter Arnold, Inc.
(© Wildlife Pictures)

Photographs courtesy of Tony Stone Images: pp. 2 (roseate
spoonbill) (© Eastcott/Momatiuk), 27 (moray eel and cleaner
shrimp) (© Mike Severns), 28 (top left/hippopotamus) Daryl
Balfour); Animals Animals/Earth Scenes: pp. 4-5 (African el-
ephants) (© Peter Weimann), 6-7 (piglet) (© Ralph Reinhold),
8 (yellow warbler) (© Gerard Lacz), 14 (black bear) (© Robert
Winslow); Minden Pictures: pp. 9 (pelicans) (© Tim Fitzharris),
10 (shoveler duck) (© Frans Lanting), 21 (giraffe and oxpeckers)
(© Frans Lanting), 28 (bottom left/chimpanzees) (© Frans
Lanting); Bruce Coleman, Inc.: p. 12 (tsetse fly) (© Kim Taylor);
Visuals Unlimited: p. 13 (Morgan horse) (© Bill Kamin); The
National Audubon Society Collection/Photo Researchers, Inc.: pp.
17 (lion) (© Mitch Reardon), 22-23 (hippopotamus) (© Gregory
Ochocki), 25 (chisel-tooth wrasse and cleaner wrasse) (© Allan
Power), 28 (right/African elephant) (© Mark Phillips); Peter Arnold,
Inc.: pp. 18-19 (chimpanzees) (© Gunter Ziesler)

Library of Congress Cataloging-in-Publication Data

Sayre, April Pulley.
Splish! Splash! animal baths/April Pulley Sayre.
p. cm.
Includes bibliographical references (p.).
Summary: Describes how different animals, such as elephants,
birds, horses, and fish, keep themselves clean.
ISBN 0-7613-1821-6 (lib. bdg.)
1. Animal behavior Juvenile literature. 2. Baths Juvenile
literature. [1. Animals—Habits and behavior. 2. Baths.]
I. Title.
QL751.5.S42   2000
591.56'3—dc21   99-42749   CIP

Published by The Millbrook Press, Inc.
2 Old New Milford Road
Brookfield, Connecticut 06804
www.millbrookpress.com
All rights reserved.

Printed in Hong Kong
Copyright © 2000 by April Pulley Sayre
All rights reserved
5 4 3 2 1